MW00891826

Published by New Leaf Interactive Media, Inc.

Copyright © 2011 by Dean Rathje

All Rights Reserved

ISBN-13: 978-1461173656

ISBN-10: 1461173655

BISAC: Poetry/General

Country of Publication: United States

Publication Date: May 11, 2011

PRINTED IN THE UNITED STATES OF AMERICA

Milk & Honey

POEMS BY

Dean Rathje

New Leaf
INTERACTIVE MEDIA

Author's Preface

This is my seventh slim volume of poetry. The effort to achieve poetic voice, to move the reader, to make the hairs stand up on the neck, to illuminate and reflect and explore—these are the tasks of the poet. My writing of poetry is complemented by my writing of music lyrics. It's often seemed to me that some of my better poetry appears as song lyrics. So, in this volume, I've allowed myself to include poems which also appear as lyrics in my music.

Dean Rathje
Ely, Iowa
May, 2011

Two Minds

It seems I'm of two minds.
The small mind attends to daily things
like food and shelter and taking care of cars.
That mind works well in its own sphere.
But it doesn't seem able to deal with
larger matters like creating work
and income and hunting for success.
That's the work of the greater mind.
Between these two minds is I think
a sort of discontinuity.

The small mind, when it tries
to deal with larger questions,
starts to have problems.
It ratchets and fumes. It succumbs
to fear and exasperation. It's out of its depth.
The great mind, which is visionary in nature
and delights in creativity, philosophy, religion,
literature, the arts and humanities, does not
want to be answerable to
the small mind of daily concerns.

The great mind is up in the clouds.
It senses the state of humanity,
gauges itself against great dreams,
and undertakes honorific work.
It doesn't want to be bothered

with particulars, but focuses only
on inspiration and where that leads.
The small mind, the earth mind,
wants to call the great mind down
from the clouds and put it to work
doing menial tasks. The great mind
sees only danger in this. To touch
earth would make it lose its greatness.
The sky appears to touch the earth
at the horizon, but the sky never
really touches the earth.

The great mind is ungrounded,
except in itself. The small mind
is too grounded, and in being too
grounded, grinds itself down with
work and worry, while the great
mind, like an eagle, soars above.
The small mind feeds on the corn
it finds on the ground. It drinks
the rainwater it finds in rivulets
on the earth. The great mind
feeds on love. It's love that
sends it soaring.

What is grounded follows
the curve of the earth, round
and round until, exhausted,
it falls to the ground and

becomes one with it. What is
groundless and fathomless
and unspeakable exists always,
before and after the earth,
before and after existence,
before and after time.

This Little House

What's going on in this little house?
Father puts all his time into ventures,
some of which succeed, and some of
which seem capable of success, but a
success so dim and distant that it may
be many years in the making.

Mother is worrying her day away at work.
She's hemmed herself into a corner,
and there doesn't seem to be any way out.
Son is making his first steps toward career,
but keeps veering into distraction, and
rarely rouses himself to get up and about.

Each has his anxieties, each his distractions,
each his hopes and fears. Mother would like
to give up her day job, retire, and possibly
move out of state. Father would like to retire,
or even go back to work. He's tired of his
venturing life and wishes only for warmth,
safety, and an easy way of life. There's nothing
harder than not working.

What is Sonny hoping for? Does he have a
plan for his life? He's a bright lad, but stubborn;
talented, but lazy; healthy, but inert. He needs

to grow into independence from his parents. He needs to find the passion of his life and follow it. He needs to dream a great dream and live it.

At dinner-time, we gather together and break bread. If fear or envy or some other strong emotion tries to get the upper hand, we send it packing. This is our time to be peaceful and happy, to cook together, to be together in love. Then we're back to our own distractions—the TV, the computer, the past.

Singing the Wound

I, the Wound Bearer,
am allowed to sing the wound.
I, the Wounded Innocent,
am allowed to speak the truth.

The wound is old. It goes
back to before my beginning.
To heal the wound takes a lifetime.
Drawing poison from the wound
takes every fiber of my being.

I work and live only marginally,
My being is devoted to the
healing of the wound.

Perhaps I am the wound.

Son of a wounding father,
son of a beaten mother,
victim of depression and fraud,
I am the bread others eat,
the song others sing.

What others consider happiness,
I consider to be only distraction.
I allow myself none of the pleasures
for which the others live.

These pleasures are purchased
at a price I'm unwilling to pay.
To have these pleasures, they
must sign their souls away.

When I was born, my mother
said, "This one is mine." My
father flew into a jealous rage
which has lasted throughout my life.

Jealous people are the bane of my life.

I have endured being kicked in my
mother's womb. I have endured abuse
by my father in the cradle. I have
endured being beaten as a son.
I have endured being slandered and
libeled as a man. I have endured the
loss of a trust. I have endured betrayal
by men of the cloth, both the black cloth
and the red. I have been declared deceased.

I have been picked over by the ravens.
I have been slandered by the jackasses.
I have seen my bright fortunes usurped.

This is all the music of the wound.

What medicine might heal such a wound?
The medicine of singing has been known
to be effective. The medicine of writing
has been known to help. The medicine
of meditation reduces inflammation.

The healing of the wound is the end of time.

The wound is the rupture between man
and God, engendered by the beginning
of time, exacerbated by the centuries,
inflamed by war, incensed by prayer,
placated by poetry, disguised by art.

The end of time is my royal beginning.

Perhaps I am the wound. Jealous people
are the bane of my life. This is all the
music of the wound. The healing of the
wound is the end of time. The end of time
is my royal beginning.

In the beginning of a thing, its end is
implied. In the end of a thing, its
beginning is erased. Erasure is the
end of the wound.

Hen Wen

Hen Wen, a huge old sow,
lived in a valley in Cornwall.
Hen Wen was to have a litter,
prophesied to bring a fall.

Arthur gathered a group of men
following her by her scent.
She burrowed along
till she came to the sea,
landing at last in Gwent.

Coll the swineherd rode the hog
holding her by her bristles.
She dragged him along
through sea and land,
gorse and grime and thistles.

At Maes Gwenith
in the county of Gwent,
three grains of wheat
and three bees she left.

She may as well
have left them money —
their products now are
wheat and honey.

Then she went to Dyved,
where this sow that was so big
left them a grain of barley
and a little pig.

From this sow
whose tail was curled
come the best pigs and barley
in all the world.

On she went to Arvon,
where she left a little cat.
Coll the swineherd
tried to drown it,
but he did not
succeed at that.

Hen Wen means "old white."
She wouldn't give up
without a fight.
This sow, the biggest
in all creation,
is really the goddess
of inspiration.

The Peaceable Kingdom

We seek wisdom to avoid pain.
We may be enlightened beings,
or, like amoebae, simply respond
to light and dark, pleasure and pain.

The pleasures of the enlightened life
include the ability to take delight
in the simplest of things: making
food for friends, sharing time with
someone in need, earning a living
with our given talents, raising children
who share our sensibilities or some
part of them, gardening, music,
and love in all its forms:

Erotic love, altruistic love, filial
devotion, the love of children and
the old, the love of the people with
whom we share our lives, the love
of community and neighbors, the
love of country and the earth.

God lives within each of us,
prompting us to love each other.
The white light of identity with
God is at the heart of each of us.

Or, if you prefer, the emptiness
of God and the loneliness of God
are at the heart of each of us,
moving us with need toward
each other.

How can we treat ourselves and
each other in ways that ennoble
and satisfy us? Leaving another
ill-used diminishes our well-being.
Are we enlightened beings, living
in the peaceable kingdom, or just
wild dogs, fighting over every scrap?
Our animal natures exist. To be
fully human, we must temper our
animal natures with wisdom and
discretion.

We live in an age of zealotry.
Each is zealous for his own cause,
his own ego, his own territory.
It is an age of fanaticism which
begs for moderation. We seek
the relief of self-abandonment.
The self becomes a maze of
rationalizations, a mass of
inherent contradictions. The
self is no longer habitable. The

house is on fire, so the inhabitants
flee for higher ground.

It is on this higher ground that
wisdom begins. We can't flee
back to a burning home. We
don't want to re-enter the maze
of suffering. We wish to stay
on this hill above the plain,
where the battles of the flesh
rage on without pity or remorse.
We wish to look down with
care on the remains of the lives
we have left behind, their troubles,
their worries, their utter lack of
calm.

The horses of passion, ridden by
the overlords of ego, are now the
horses which draw the plows of
peace and contentment. Here we
plant the seeds of wisdom and
justice, temperance and love.

The Youth

This fire we feel, to do and be:
what happens when it burns out?
A cold old soul lives in the ashes of regret,
staring out the window of his self-complacency.

This love we feel, and share and live:
what happens when we cease to feel it?
A lonely woman lives in the fires of despair,
burning in that eternal flame of lost love.

Springing up between them, the youth:
callow at times, not yet tempered by
the daily weight of work, still in his
youthful bloom of optimism and hope.

How can we draw forward from his soul
the fire and passion and energy he needs
to find and do his life's work? We worry
that he'll never leave home.

One night, when he and I were fighting,
I saw him standing in the driveway,
in his coat, near his car, as if to leave,
and nearly wept.

Raising a son in love is impossible.
They'll say you have no knack for
discipline. You've let him grow soft.
He'll end up as a murderer or thief.

Yet the murderers and thieves I know
got that way, not from too little discipline,
nor too much love, but just the opposite.

It's Tough to Be Me

It's tough to be me
on a given day,
with so much baggage
that's put in play.

it's tough to be me
and look at my son,
who has the same problems
I cut my teeth on.

It's tough to grow old
and not know the way,
to feel like you're wandering
every day.

It's tough to go on
when your parents are dead,
and knowing your own tomb
lies dead ahead.

It's tough to get up
and go on with your day,
when you feel that your fortunes
are skidding sideways.

It's tough to relent
when your work here is done.
just give up your hatred
and go on in love.

Just a Harp

I'm just a harp being played by the wind,
a tool of fate, a fool of God,
an instrument of salvation,
an open window to love,
a way others may take
but which I myself have forgotten.
A lonesome, long and bumpy road,
a path of repentance and forgiveness,

A road of insight and wisdom,
a scenic route of passion,
a stormy road of courage,
a hill beyond the city,
a tree beyond the town,
a footpath wide enough for one,
a way of love and yet of struggle,

An open wound, revealing health,
an open mind, reflecting God.
There's no escaping suffering,
no way to love except through death.

Long ago, I left the common road
to pursue the path of wisdom.
Long ago, I forsook the common road
to face my fears and embrace them.

Long ago, I ceased looking at myself
as I felt that I should be,
Long ago, I accepted myself as I am
and just gave up the struggle.

I took the scenic route,
and I've become the scenic route.
I took the way of self-forgetting
and have remembered something
much better than myself.

Just for You

All day long I've waited to see you.
My work is like idle play.
I walk through the meadows.
I put my toys away.

A certain bird
whose name I've never known
comes to greet me.
Those who know its name
are men of science.
I'm a man of faith.

Born of cosmic residue
after the comet's last passing,
I've come to relieve mankind
    of its toil.
. I come as a gardener
a lover of all that's old,
a questioner, a prodder,
a tinker and a trader.

All the faces of men and women
are like the face of God to me.
All of them spring from one source,
and near that source, that stream,
I linger lying in the grass,

twisting a tuft of rye, singing softly,
luxuriating in the luxury of existence,
plowing the soft earth, farming its farms
raining its rains, harvesting its harvests,
bringing forth from the living earth
all the contents of its possibility.

All day long I've waited to see your face.
All my life I've longed to feel your love.
All night long I'm singing like a dove,
singing softly in the waning light of day,
lying in the grass of my remembrance,
fondling my memories,
reaching into my harmonies,
licking at the edges of my fantasies,
driving surely and deeply
into all that's good and true.

All day long I've waited just for you.

Michelangelo

A sculptor took an old stone block,
dark and weathered with age,
and made a beautiful drawing
with a pencil on a page.

He sets himself to carve the stone
and make the image come.
His passion is the instrument.
His heart is filled with love.

Days and weeks and years go by,
unbeknownst to him.
His hair is turning gray now.
His eyes are growing dim.

His other works line the city streets.
His fame is distantly spread.
But this piece is his final one.
He doesn't need the bread

Writing in his journal,
he talks about his work.
He regrets so much about his life.
He goes a little berserk.

At night he works by candlelight.
The forms and shapes appear.
He hopes he'll live to finish it,
weeks or months or years.

Sooner or later we all make peace
with the harvester of souls,
who puts an end to all our plans,
our works, our dreams, our goals.

May you die doing what you love,
and may it bear your stamp,
even if it's unfinished
when the reaper dims your lamp.

My Favorite Things

A package of windmill cookies and a bottle of milk.
In the winter, long underwear made of silk.

The first warm day of spring, and the last warm day of fall.
Some photos of travel trips hung upon my wall.

A long spring with intermittent rains.
A long drive across the Great Plains.

A long autumn with majestic colorful trees.
On a hot day, a cool, persistent breeze.

A day with nothing whatsoever to do.
A talk with my Mom and Dad about you.

A good book, a cup of coffee, and a cigarette.
A chance to pay off all your niggling debts.

A long talk with an old friend who's deep in despair.
New socks and jeans and sweaters and underwear.

A long and winding country road nearby.
Thanksgiving dinner with turkey and pumpkin pie.

Music that speaks directly to your heart.
A deep and abiding love of human art.

Faces, hands, and bodies touching well.
A chance to redeem yourself from the depths of hell.

The sound of the autumn wind sighing through the trees.
Freedom throughout your life from pain and disease.

A chance to make an excellent working wage.
Excellent health and income in middle age.

Living long enough to become a sage.
Wealth and many children in old age.

Love in all its forms, on a given day.
Dinner with friends at a trendy little café.

A roasted duck served over oyster dressing.
Hearing a little child recite the blessing.

Travel through an unknown place or land.
A pint of stout and a talk with your oldest friend.

Any form of religious or filial devotion.
Any body of water: river, lake, or ocean.

An afternoon talk on the telephone with you.
A month or two of studying the blues.

Old love letters found in a family chest.

Seeing someone you love when you're depressed.

A place in the country that just belongs there.

Sitting around the fire in scuffed-up Adirondack chairs.

A wraparound porch on an Iowa farmhouse frame.

A chance to score the winning run in a game.

Good strong coffee and fresh banana bread.

Canvas sails seamed with silken thread.

Friends gathered in the yard, with their instruments out.

Pies and cakes and coffee in the house.

A song that just comes together, with you as the instrument..

Another song, of which this one is the remnant.

The realization that life is extremely brief.

The sunshine of love beaming down through the shadows of grief.

Nemesis

Nemesis hold an hourglass,
in her other hand, a sword.
She hovers over each of us,
like the vengeance of the Lord.

The hourglass is our time on earth.
We learn to bide it well.
The sword is retribution.
She casts us into hell.

She metes out our just deserts.
Each one gets his share.
Those who grab for more, though,
had better have a care.

The right proportion she defends,
and hubris won't allow.
Balance is her watchword,
inexorable her vow.

Adamantine her bridles,
insolence she can't stand.
Frivolous mortals fear her.
Watch yourselves, my friends.

Only Passion

We come from the womb
trailing the warm, wet past.
We live in that amnios for
twenty years or so, until
one day it dries up, and we
become adults.

We keep yearning for that
warm, wet stuff of which
we came. We look for it in
booze and drugs, religion,
meditation and art, in sex
and other mortal pleasures.

Do we find it? The long terrain
of life, the long walking toward
the sun, is weakening, death-
defying, an act against gravity.
To maintain posture and poise
requires a great deal of focus.

Within us, there is, from birth,
some passion, the realization
of which is joy, the denial of
which is sorrow. To find and
live that passion is all we must
do. Nothing else matters.

Ship of Love

Beyond the valley of self-doubt
rises the mountain of music.
Along the river of song
grow the trees of success.

Deep in the woods of despair,
among old boulders of the past,
lie the remnants of a family
that lost its soul to greed.

Along the trail of love,
lie many little oases —
stopping points for pleasure,
refuge from darkness
for the night.

Along the road of loving
lies remembrance,
golden moments shining
in the litter of the past.

Far along the trail of life lies money.
A ship heavy laden has been
a long time coming.
Brigands and thieves have
riven her with spears.
Dead men hang from her sides.

Dingies and rowboats
lie capsized in her wake.
A pirate ship that lay
   across her path
has been cleft in two.

The ship of victory cruises.
big, heavy, and deep with gold,
into the harbor of love.

,

The Emperor

Old stone blocks, piles of rocks,
moving them one at a time,
building a palace for the emperor,
some kind of holy shrine.

The people move the stones
while the emperor lives in fear.
We see an armed rebellion.
His end is drawing near.

The emperor lives in pleasure
while the people live in dread
He's posted fifteen bodyguards
around his pleasure bed.

He has his choice of concubines,
a different one each night.
To them it is a terror.
To him it's a delight.

His kingdom stretches on and on,
across the storied plain.
On one end we see moon and stars,
on the other wind and rain.

He's taken up his retinue
to view his holdings fair.
His friends are few and far between,
his enemies everywhere.

One night in the desert,
when all his pleasure's spent,
he's set upon by outcasts,
who set fire to his tent.

His concubines run screaming
off into the night,
While the emperor turns to cinders
and his horses all take flight.

The Everlasting Blues

It's easy to fall in and out of love,
to spend your life doing meaningless work,
to struggle toward what appears like success
but really rings hollow and makes you berserk.

You can work toward that fine patina later,
polishing your stones on mama's shoes,
pushing your parents into nirvana
and giving yourself the everlasting blues.

In the honesty zone there's no place for lies.
The judge and jury are in for a surprise.
You can read a man or beast by studying its eyes.
You can even crack the syndicate
if you're in the right disguise.

How do you know the right path when you're on it?
How do you know love when it stares you in the face?
How can you divine the odor of perfection,
Unless you see yourself without disgrace?

See your soul is as it was, unbargained,
freed from all the stings and arrows thrown.
No longer is your happiness postponed.

As the gates of heaven open inward,
the gate of hell is claiming its own prey.
you're learning to sing with your own voice,
collecting those thoughts that went astray.

The Farmer and the Wolf

A skinny wolf,
hungry from many days
of ranging on the plains,
comes upon a baby lamb,
playing in the grass,
knowing nothing,
fearing nothing.

The lamb's mother
hovers nearby. She
smells the wolf and
then hears it. She
makes a loud cry
to alert the herd,
and the farmer,
ever watchful of his flock,
grabs his gun and
runs to the pasture.

The wolf comes
crashing out of the woods,
toward the flock.
Just then, the farmer
comes wheeling out
from the barn, lifts
the rifle to his shoulder,
and drops the wolf

with a single shot.
He burns the wolf
in a pile of scrap wood,
giving thanks for his lambs
and also for his hens.
Tomorrow, perhaps,
there will be another wolf.
But for now, all is well.

A higher, stronger fence?
More lights around the farm?
What will keep a wolf at bay
and protect my flocks from harm?
A hired man, wandering the
woods nearby? Should I
cut back the timber for
half a mile around, and plant
a barrier hedge, too thick
for a wolf to creep through?

These thoughts, and others
like them, occupy the mind
of the good farmer. He has
built up his grazing flock by
being vigilant, by breeding
for good qualities, by being
astute at the market, and
above all, by keeping
predators at bay.

The Furies

The furies fly around your head,
filling you with fear and dread.
Mother murder, father murder,
killing son or wife —
the angry ones will follow you
and curse your through your life.

Born from drops of godly blood,
born from womb of night,
when mortals swear a lying oath,
they're bound to set things right.
Personifying the angry dead,
they make the living cringe,
until the oath that's made with blood
causes minds to come unhinged.

If you swear a lying oath,
or murder those you love,
beware the pecking birds of fate,
Erinyes from above.

The Inner Pair

In one sense, I've led a happy life—
pretty healthy, drinking a little wine.
In another sense, I've led a tragic life,
deprived of what should rightfully be mine.

My mother-self has always been my happy self—
loved, adored, promoted, cared for, esteemed.
My father-self has always been my hurting self,
victimized by jealousy and greed.

Imagine being each of those two people—
the happy one always trying to achieve,
and the hurting one always feeling victimized,
always trying too hard to believe.

This inner pair, this household,
this set of archetypes,
seems to have a hard time coexisting—
just as my parents fought,
and my father used his fists,
and me all of this conflict resisting.

He was just a party boy
who married a Catholic girl.
I'm not sure he really wanted to be a dad.
She made him join the Church,
and he hooked her on the booze.

That's why you might see her
looking a little sad.

Kids who grow up
in this kind of home
try to make it right
by being perfect saints.
But then they get hit in the head
by a dad on booze and pills,
and the mother goes out
making her complaints.

The police and the church
confront the abusive dad.
The mother swears that she will
up and leave him.
He doesn't like authorities
telling him what to do.

Will he tell the truth now?
Will anyone even believe him?

The River of Song

The river of story, the river of song,
so deep and dread, so winding and long.
You never step into that same river twice.
In the summer it flows. In the winter it's ice.

Stories of love and of youthful demise
make us laugh and despair and bring tears to our eyes.
Stories of wandering, leaving the home,
pilgrimages made to the scepter and throne.

One life goes up and another goes down.
One touches evil, another the crown.
One snaps like a stick and goes into despair.
Another stacks bricks and lives with great care.

The rich and the poor, the wise and the cruel,
those who eat *foie gras* and those who eat gruel.
A grueling fight to the death with a foe,
and a nod and a twitter from those in the know.

A young man who's making his way to the king
is attacked by three highwaymen formed in a ring.
He's tied to a tree and is made to cry,
then he's slashed through the chest and left to die.

A mother who's tending her baby with care
is raped by her husband who's watching her there.

The baby goes crying without his milk,
while the father retreats in pajamas of silk.

Those who float down this river see forests of trees,
but I who see deeper see the human disease:
envy and murder, rape and abuse.
It's no wonder the heart soon dies of disuse.

Repentance

The work of my father's repentance
is now the work at hand.

When you've used your best son
as a scapegoat, loading your sins
on him, beating him, stealing his
money, stealing his mail, keeping
him from his mother's love, then
how can you tally this at the end
of your life?

I should never have had to work
a day in my life. Money put aside
for me should have sailed me
through life's straits. But he put
himself between me and prosperity,
between me and love, between me
and my mother, and fouled that
relationship with lies.

The sum of those lies is the loss
of my faith. He has made a good
man look bad, a bright man look
stupid, a happy man seem dead.
His abuse of my character, in the
service of fraud, has done me
harm beyond telling. He has tried

to make himself seem great at
my expense.

How does that tally at the end?
How does that line up when it's
time to meet your Maker? How
can we calculate the losses I
have sustained on his account?
Perhaps, in the end, all his lies
are exposed, his abuse of me
brought under scrutiny. Perhaps
he will finally confess.

Or simply gild himself with my
money into the grave.

How can he have allowed
the others to live off my
trusts? How can he have
abrogated two trusts and
numerous inheritances?
How can he have stolen
my name, my mail, my
identity?

How can he have done
all this, and still pretend
to have a soul?

A certain perversity of
character is evident here.

From the kink in his mind
about me forms a conspiracy
of fraud and yes hatred, with
me as its object. What have
I done to deserve this kind
of abuse, starting at my birth
and continuing to this day?

Because of him, I have had
to watch myself, each day,
to ensure the seeds of this
hatred do not enter my soul.
I have had to keep myself
from violent anger, drunk-
enness, and other forms of
evil. I have had to break in
myself the pattern of what
he has done to me.

This has been the work of
my life, not to be like him.
Not to aggrandize myself
at another's expense. Not
to play the great man while
letting a good son go hurting.
Not to put the shadow of

my animal nature on another.
Not to harm the innocent,
nor glorify the wicked. Not
to bring another to the point
of despair.

Instead, I have sought out
others who are at the point
of despair, and tried to help.
I've looked into his heart,
and into mine, and tried to
find the cause of his hatred.

His life and mine have both
come to a fine point, his to
the point of repentance, mine
to the point of creating my
life's work. The substance of
his repentance is the fuel of
my creating.

It is hard to plant a mustard
seed in flinty soil, difficult to
see it wither from lack of love.

He has stolen my substance,
my name, my love of my mother.
His jealousy of me begins in
my cradle and ends in his grave.

Now he's willing to give up a
little to buy his own funeral.
He wants to go out as a good
man, with honors. Yet it seems
he was really a coward and a
traitor, willing to betray his
own son for money, from petty
jealousy.

Do we honor him now? Pity
him? Forgive him? Forgiveness
comes only after complete
confession. Can a man live
an evil life and then repent
between the stirrup and the
ground?

What I have achieved in my
life has been through sheer
effort. He has taken away the
means of my salvation and left
me to suffer the agonies of his
hatred.

I dream of a loving father,
which I have tried to become
to my own children. I dream

of a father who's behind me
at every turn in life, helping
me toward my best outcome.

He has reimbursed himself
for the cost of my upbringing.
He held money for me to
marry and be educated, but
never gave me any of it, even
though it didn't come from him.

He kicked me in the womb,
beat me as a child, and vowed
to murder me in cold blood.

I have done nothing but
honor my mother and him,
from the day of my birth
until now. I have been the
good son all parents crave,
the one with high honors,
the one who is spoken well
of, the one who has gone out
of his way to celebrate his
parents, the one whom
everybody loves.

A beating in the head at six
has left me with an ear that,

fifty years later, still has
bouts of ringing. My life has
been an endless cringing
from that blow.

Before the law, he portrayed
me as a miscreant, a lout, a man
not worthy of a trust. And then
purloined my life's income, putting
it into his own name. And has vowed
that I will not receive a penny of
income while he lives.

This is just the opposite of how a
good father would behave. He has
sought to undermine my reputation.
He has sought to undermine my
career. He has left me rudderless
in life. He has used my name in vain.
He has written letters pretending
to be me.

Did my mother allow this to happen?
I think he undermined her too. She
was the one who brought the Church
into his life, something he never
liked. She was the one who brought
me into his life. The third party in
any good marriage is God. He didn't

want God in his marriage.
Imagine a postmaster who steals
his son's mail. Imagine him stealing
checks from that mail, and burning
or shredding everything else.
Imagine him paying a series of
postal employees, over the years,
to pluck all checks and letters of
honor and offers of employment
and anything else of value from
my mail.

Imagine him using my money to
raise and educate and house my
sister's daughters. Imagine her
becoming his conspirator in fraud
and character assassination.
Imagine the two of them killing
my mother and then rushing,
breathless as two lovers, to the
attorney's office to amend her
will *post mortem*.

Thus does his jealousy of me
lead to another generation of
hate crimes, and then another.

What will it take to bring this
conspiracy down? How will

this story be told, and by whom?
How will retribution be made?
Can we put out the fire of fraud,
and also stamp out each ember?
His hatred of my mother, his
hatred of the Church, and his
hatred of me are all the same.

If you choose to be like her,
then you'll get the same beating
I gave her!

And you'll still treat me
as sweetly as if I were the
best father on earth.

CPSIA information can be obtained
at www.ICGtesting.com
Printed in the USA
BVOW03s0834191217
503197BV00001B/131/P

9 781461 173656